THE ALMANAC

THE
ALMANAC

poems

STEVE STRAIGHT

CURBSTONE BOOKS
NORTHWESTERN UNIVERSITY PRESS
EVANSTON, ILLINOIS

Curbstone Books
Northwestern University Press
www.nupress.northwestern.edu

Printed in the United States of America

10 9 8 7 6 5 4 3 2 1

Library of Congress Cataloging-in-Publication Data
Straight, Steve, 1954–
    The almanac : poems / Steve Straight.
        p. cm.
    ISBN 978-0-8101-2835-4 (pbk. : alk. paper)
    I. Title.
    PS3619.T73A78 2012
    811.6—dc23

                                    2012011858

For Marian

CONTENTS

Acknowledgments   *ix*

Only Connect   *3*

1

The Horse Does Not Know It Is in a Movie   7

How to Catch a Fly   9

The Language of Trees   11

ESL Dog   13

Remote   15

Punctuation   17

Universe in B-flat   19

Retreat   21

An Italian Farmer Explains to Us the Meaning of Life   23

The Land of Nod   25

Scout   27

God   29

ST RAGE   30

Monkey Mind   31

Endangered Species   34

How to Survive Right-Wing Extremism   35

Novena   36

The Flag of Cucumber   39

Memoir	43
More	48
Plasticville	50
Honorary Junior Black Panther	53
Panning	56
General Lee	58
Grief	60
Birthday	61
The Country of Bed	62
The Paddle	64
The News	66
Development	68
Good Days	69
The Art of Memory	71
The Next-to-Last Poem	73
The Almanac	74

Grateful acknowledgment is made to the editors of the following journals, where several of these poems, some in slightly different form, first appeared:

Common Ground Review: "ESL Dog," "The Next-to-Last Poem," "Universe in B-flat"

Connecticut Review: "The Almanac"

Freshwater: "God," "The Language of Trees"

Teaching English in the Two-Year College: "Punctuation," v 36.3, March 2009; "Remote," v 37.3, March 2010; "ST RAGE," v 39.2, December 2011; "How to Catch a Fly," v 40.2, December 2012. Copyright by the National Council of Teachers of English. Reprinted by permission.

Theodate: "The Horse Does Not Know It Is in a Movie"

War, Literature & the Arts: "The Flag of Cucumber"

My thanks to Sandy Taylor and Judy Doyle of Curbstone Press, Rennie Mc-Quilkin, Jeff Sommers, John Stanizzi, Mike and Mariana DiRaimo, Noreen and Darius Kirk, Flo and Tim Stella, all my colleagues at Manchester Community College who have invited me into their classes, and all the friends who gave these their first listen. Thanks especially to my new friends at Northwestern.

THE ALMANAC

Only Connect

Let me pour you a cup of coffee with milk,
or without, whatever way you like it.
Let me add a piece of toast, though
Lord knows I have no idea what kind.
Whole wheat? Rye? Cinnamon swirl?
Even butter for the toast seems like a risk;
it's too dangerous to suggest a jam.

Dear reader, I want to connect with you
right off, find some common ground,
not chance waiting until the final line
when our philosophies coalesce like pudding.

For I know how tenuous this whole affair is,
me dumping the contents of my consciousness
right on your table—wood? Formica?—and
sorting it right in front of you
for little acorn tops of truth in among
the lint, paper clips, and pennies.

I know I've already lost some of you—
tea drinkers, orange juicers, bagel mavens—
and some of you are hanging on by a thread,
waiting for "cottage by the lake" or
"when my kids were in diapers" or
"clematis tendrils looping the iron trellis."

I know myself when Heidegger enters the poem,
or the musical *Cats,* the page is half-turned
right there, and if the poet doesn't swing back
to my territory, I have magazines unread
beside me, and plenty of old photograph albums
to thumb through.

I know there is no changing you, reader,
that I can only hope to add another flavor,
put another song into the rotation.
But if I can establish that rapport of like minds,
adjust the knob to exactly your frequency,
then you might follow me
into the dark forest of memory
or onto the carnival ride of hypothesis,
or even right off the cliff of surprise.

1

The Horse Does Not Know It Is in a Movie

The horse does not know it is in a movie,
I am sometimes reminded,
especially in a close-up, when
all the other characters are removed
from the shot, and it is just a horse
eating hay, oblivious to the gaffers
and best boys and bright lights
outside its stall, not Pie,
the horse that wins the Grand National
with Elizabeth Taylor astride,
but probably Sam, or Big Red,
a little annoyed by all the fuss
until the hay arrived.

Nor did any of the Lassies
know they were television stars,
I have to remember,
the audience at home hanging on every
cocked ear, every suddenly rigid stance
when Timmy was in danger,
waiting for June Lockhart to say again,
"What is it, girl?"
It wasn't anything, except a young collie
playing that game again,
doing those tricks for Rudd Weatherwax,
attentive to his tics and hand signals
as he stood off camera with a treat.

Now that I think of it, those cows
I saw on top of the Cliffs of Moher,
in County Clare, have no idea
they are Irish cows, characters
in the long-running, bumpy play
called Ireland, have no notion
of religion or history or any of our powers
to name and distort the world.
They only ruminate
on the sacrament of grass.

And if I am perfectly honest about it,
most days I do not know
that I am on a stage,
do not notice my Weatherwax
in the wings raise one finger
to arouse that memory from my childhood,
or wag his left foot to bring that scowl
of recurring anxiety to my face,
or summon that metaphor
by cocking his head to the right.
Most of the time I think I'm just a man
who comes up with these things
all on his own.

How to Catch a Fly

Wait until the fly is still,
preferably on a surface
with space on either side of it,
as we all would like to exist,
even better if it is occupied
with its fly yoga, passing
one leg over its head
and then another. Now
bring your hand up gradually
behind the fly and pause.

Do not try to catch the fly
where it is, or you will catch
a perfect handful of air.
You must catch the fly
where it will be, the future fly,
the fly one second from now.
This is one lesson of desire.

So, then, when you are ready
(sometimes the fly will sense this
and stop all motion)
swoop your hand over the fly in
one clean motion ending with
a gently closed fist in the air,
with thumb on top,
then feel the fly buzz inside
against the walls.

Appreciate for a moment
the coevolutionary arc
that all of natural history
has conspired to achieve
this intersection of species.
A sigh here is optional.

At this point you might
surprise a yawning friend,
or roll the fly on the counter like dice,
but better to open a door or window
and release the fly back into the present,
back into the cool night air.

The Language of Trees

Supposedly, a special plant flowers only on Midsummer Eve,
and the person who picks it can understand the language of trees.

When I discovered it in my flashlight's beam
deep in the island's woods at the base of a giant white pine,
an impossible orchid that had to be the cure to something,
I heard with the first whiff of its earthy perfume
what sounded like the chatter of saplings nearby,
and when I held it to my nose came the awareness
of an invisible music that has been playing all along.

I realized then that we have all heard hints before,
like foreign words that come from similar roots,
the quaking aspen in a breeze like a flock
of Japanese women giggling behind their hands
of pale leaves, the sharp cry of an old limb
being amputated by a gust of wind,
the sighs of spruces sagging under the weight of snow.

As I inhaled my comprehension sharpened,
and I could make out discussions of climate
and weather, the sacred work of squirrels,
and what seemed to be a kind of religion
based on lightning. A cedar told the story
of being astonished by the texture of a bear,
a birch at the edge of the water described the moonlit view.
The dead at their feet were cherished as if alive,
ants and beetles slowly working them
into mulch and then to soil.

I can't say I really understood all I could hear,
perhaps because human evolution is in the teething stage,
or I was just getting used to sixty-seven words for bark,
but even with all the trees around me the woods
were quieter, the conversation gentler
than you might expect, and I noticed the older,
taller trees, their bark darkened and thickened,
said hardly a word, as if they understood
how language fails us
and spent their days listening to the wind.

ESL Dog

for Sue Purdy, Bailey, and Darwin

Of course it's his second language;
anyone can hear that in the pitiful way
he pronounces the word "chow." We see it
in his frustration, standing in one place,
legs slightly splayed, repeating the same word
over and over, as if saying it louder will
finally make us understand.

We've tried patiently to teach him,
playing our tapes of phonics with a golden
biscuit perched on top of the speaker,
or working on verbs out in Nature,
the source of all verbs, but pretty soon
he'll get distracted by a big ant or
a leaf tumbling across the lawn in a breeze
and go bounding off. . . .

His comprehension is, of course,
much better than his speech. He knows
any number of nouns for food and travel,
has learned the shame of "Bad dog,"
the caution behind "No," and all
of the common imperatives. But if
we get talking above a crawl of words,
it all goes right over his head, and
he'll look up at us with those brown eyes,
cock his head slightly, and then we know
to speak . . . real . . . slow.

Truly, he's done so well with a whimper
at the door, a belly exposure, or a nose
under your wrist while you're reading the paper,
it's no wonder he hasn't mastered the gerund,
or subject-verb agreement, or even articles.
As long as he gets his point across with
body language and a few syllables, what's
his incentive to learn more? And his accent,
my god, he'll never shed that.

Remote

Halfway through my lecture
on the secrets to writing a good essay,
I realize one of my students in the back row
whose head is angled as if studying his thigh
is actually checking his cell phone for a message
or perhaps even watching a movie

and I see now that many of my students,
sullen, passive, and unprepared today,
seem really pissed off that the remote control
that would change me to a show they like
is somehow missing, are angry no mouse
at their fingertips clicks me into hyperspace,
not even a volume control on their desks
can mute me as I drone on and on
about some product they don't want.

Or am I their employer, forcing them
to bag my ideas in paper or plastic
with a smile, not letting them use the bathroom
during this eighty-minute sweatshop,
this retail prison offering no clear paycheck,
no vision of middle-class bliss
for which they trade these grindstone days.

Or worse, since many are so young,
perhaps I am just a parent, telling them

the essay better be home by eleven,
with plenty of gas in it, and no clutter,
to pick up their run-ons and fragments
after themselves, and they listen to me
as they stare at the door to the rest of their lives.

Punctuation

Do not place a period
where God has placed a comma.
— GRACIE ALLEN

Seeing the giant banner in front of the church,
I think of all the punctuation marks
that litter the field of my mind:

commas, yes, indicating that life goes on,
or must, and I might make some sense of it
around the next bend;

semicolons winking between endless pairs
of diametrical truths that cancel each other out;

ellipses to represent all the things I used to know
but now I can't recall;

quotation marks, as I try
to enlist the wisdom of others;

the dash, for all life's punch lines and surprises, yes,
but more often in a pair, just loud parentheses
forever qualifying some point that others find so clear;

the apostrophe for all I possess,
or taking the place of all I no longer need;

the teasing caret—more information
has just arrived, sir;

the colon, promising that what comes next will follow
what has come before, only a myth, the dots more often
like the edge of a cliff;

and sometimes just when I think I have life figured out,
have found some great truth, there is
the asterisk, noting the exception or the flaw;

and so perhaps it all comes down to the question mark,
that shepherd's crook that grazes all my doubts and fears
on hillsides studded with rocks, but in among the flock
curiosity as well, the greatest impulse after love, and
by its side hope, that the exclamation point will come.

Universe in B-flat

for Ralph Maccarone

Scientists report they have discovered a black hole, 250 million
light-years from Earth, that emits a tone, said to be a B-flat,
57 octaves below our middle C.

I try to get a handle on the long numbers,
that the note is a wave 30,000 light-years across,
with an oscillation of 10 million years,
and so I sit at our piano,
a Hazelton grand from the 1930s,
where I strike the lowest clear B-flat
three octaves below middle C
with my foot on the sustain pedal,
and the waves carry the sound
throughout the house
and through the open windows
to the goldfinches clamped to their rungs on the feeder,
to the trees and grass, and down the street
to the neighbors' dogs, who prick up their ears.
As I listen to its lingering tone
in the vapor of this hot spring day
eventually I'm not sure when I've stopped hearing it
as the sound mixes with my memory of it
the way a river becomes the ocean.

My father-in-law spent all one summer once
refinishing this piano, home from his job teaching
music one town over, which he did for thirty-three years

to more than ten thousand fidgety kids,
showing three hundred at a time
how to blend their voices into one.
I was one of them. One day when I was twelve,
he rehearsed me privately for my solo as Tiny Tim,
and I complained he wanted me to sing too far
with only one breath. Without looking up
he began my song at a moderate tempo and sang
measure after measure, then page after page,
until he stopped when I knew he could go on.
"See?" he said. "You just don't know how to breathe."

I try to imagine the piano that could play
the note 432 keys below the one I am playing
and what sledgehammer would be required to sound it.
The slow curve of the piano's soundboard
would stretch eventually into a straight line
as my eyes followed the string into the distance,
a line of telephone poles marking its progress
until it vanished at a point on the horizon.
The string would extend into space, of course,
into what we've all been taught is vacuum,
silent and cold. But now the prospect
of that distant hot thin gas in Perseus
suggests that even the universe lives to breathe
and with that breath it wants to sing.

Retreat

for Carl and Marilee Dudash

Outside, in the twenty-first century, a late nor'easter
lashes the coast with hurricane winds
and slanting rain so hard it swells the rivers
over their banks and fields become lakes
stocked with astonished trout.

The storm reflects the world, it seems,
and I am happy to step inside the tiny old church,
a simple wood A with no internal beams,
where it is still the eighteenth century,
and a tall bearded man is tuning
the harpsichord he built with his own hands
in the shop beside his house. The lifted lid,
painted by his wife, reveals a motif
of birds and flowers and the motto *canto ergo sum.*

After the small congregation assembles,
the soprano takes us deeper into the past
as she sings Purcell's seventeenth-century nymphs
and shepherds to life, urging them to come away,
as we have, and we can imagine they do
come in from the grove, from their sporting and play,
and lounge with us among the pews,
and even the sheep nestle in a bunch by the altar,
their gentle eyes closed, all of us hushed
to soak in the music that God has provided,
much happier here than tossed in the tempest outside.

Here the wind is dulled but still batters the roof,
and the wooden cross hung from the rafters
by long wires sways like the pendulum
of a very old clock, moving so slowly
we may never catch up to our century again.

An Italian Farmer Explains to Us the Meaning of Life

Monteriggioni, Tuscany

We stop to wait for stragglers
on a bicycle ride through farmland
in the valley below the medieval walls.
An old farmer, in his seventies, maybe eighties,
it's hard to tell, dressed in dark blue pants
and a long-sleeved shirt on a hot day,
wearing what once might have been
his Sunday shoes, his sleeves rolled loosely
revealing large hands, forks bits of hay
from roadside mowing into a pile,
working slowly but steadily. Our guide
translates questions and answers for us.

*Yes, a long time he has worked this land. Since
he was* cosi grande, *only so tall, with his grandfather.
The farm in his family goes back very far.*

He pauses occasionally to gesticulate but keeps
working, keeps smiling. In Italian, and smiling,
it sounds and looks as if he is telling a joke.

*It is only June, he says, but these will be tomatoes,
these* fagioli—*beans—those eggplant and zucchini,
and beyond that, of course, the grapes.*

There is no secret, he says. Tutto comincia
e finisce con la terra. *Everything begins and ends
with the earth, the soil.*

He nods in the direction of a vast expanse of red
across neighboring fields as he lifts another
forkful of hay.

Can you tell me, he asks, where do those papaveri,
*those poppies, come from? What is the source
of the soybean flower, yellow as the sun?*
La terra. *Wine, the oil of olives, cheeses,
even* latte materno, *the mother's milk, he says,
can be traced to the soil. And what makes
the stone, the piazza, the church?*

*Even the faith in God, he says, is faith
in the soil. He is sure of this. And
where is the blood spilled, always?
This is the source of all sorrow and joy,
he says,*

still smiling, still working.

The Land of Nod

East of Eden, and isn't everything, now,
he turns a pile of compost with his pitchfork,
a loose, warm pile of leaves, manure, and dirt.
Like memories, sifted long enough, they lose
their separateness and become a bed for seeds.
He handles the pitchfork with ease, spinning its smooth shaft
in his calloused left hand, mindful of his work
to create the best possible soil, given its curse from God.

We don't know how long he lived,
but if he lived as long as his father, or his other brother,
Seth, he lived a long time, long enough
to take some measure of the world and find his place in it.
His days as fugitive and vagabond did pass,
and it was possible to live without seeing the face of God.
His was not the first sin, after all, and now
a flaming sword kept everyone out of Eden.

He pauses now and leans on the pitchfork.
In the distance he can see the world's first city,
which he built and named for his son.
On the wind comes the music of a harp. Nearby
the animals snort and shuffle contentedly.
Soon his wife will come out with bread and wine.
At night he will dream.

Yes, it feels sometimes as if his life were a story
being told by someone else, as if the twilight came

when some great reader turned a giant page
that blocked the sun. Yet as he reminds
his great-great-grandchildren, let no moment
define you. There is no telling what your hands
and heart can do. And may God be in your debt
for the mark you leave on the world.

Scout

From the back of the Chicago city bus
I study a man up front on the bench seat
facing the opposite side. Fat, perhaps forty,
legs slightly splayed, he keeps rubbing the fuzz
on his skull, eyeing each person who enters
with a kind of intensity that makes women
avoid him, even change their seats at the next stop.

There is no violence in his actions,
merely a compelling oddness,
and I can't help thinking
what a perfect disguise for Jesus.

He's come to take the pulse
of our humanity, to see how much
we've progressed in two millennia,
and if it's worth a second trip.
He's the advance scout for himself,
out on a reconnaissance of the spirit,
armed with the absence of money,
style, or charm.

I see other candidates almost every day,
the Down syndrome kid who tries to hug
strangers, the goofy bagger at the grocery store
who taxes everyone's patience with his friendly chatter,
the war veteran outside the Art Institute
crying softly from his wheelchair, "Help me. Help me."

Probably He is also the cranky woman
confined to her bed, the man with the accent
asking directions when we're in a rush,
perhaps even the mangy stray mutt
poking through the trash who looks up,
curious about our intentions,
suggesting grace in his own little way.

God

after Wallace Stevens

If there is a god in the house,
let her show us in magical ways,
the phone ringing with each friend
we were about to call, the lost key appearing
in the bottom of the ice cream container,
the banana for cereal that ripens in your hand.

It will take some time, of course, for us
to connect these events to god: the little bell
on the stove that dings at each act of kindness,
the Jehovah's Witness who brings back the dog—
to move ourselves beyond coincidence to belief—
the smell of gardenias whenever the computer
crashes, the birthday card from your long-dead aunt.

We seem so resistant to magic, let us hope
it won't take a downpour from the tiny cloud
over the houseplant we forgot to water, or
a sudden flock of passenger pigeons lighting
in the maple trees, or below the hill at the back
of the property the fresh sound of surf. Let us
see it before one morning standing on the lawn
is a very pale horse, nibbling the grass
covered with dew.

ST RAGE

proclaim the block letters on the brick building
we pass as the bus arrives in New York City,
and tasting the rancid steam rising up
through the grates of a civilization
past its expiration date, feeling
the tension in the air as the remaining
spoils of the natural world are divided,
seeing the politicians and the powerful
scatter whenever the lights are turned on,
I can understand why.

It's a miracle more of us don't shoot each other,
or T-bone other drivers who block our paths.
It's no wonder we feel something missing
no matter what we pour into our lives.

We may need to fill in the Os of closure,
of wholeness, ourselves, kids drawing them
in beach sand with sticks, or
special teams parachuting Os from the sky,
or even forming the Os with our own bodies,
sitting with Buddha arms, hands
cupped gently in our laps,
slowly counting to ten.

Monkey Mind

> In meditation, the busy mind
> is said to act like a monkey,
> leaping from tree to tree.

I first noticed him years ago
when I was doing *zazen,*
sitting on my *zafu,*
gazing but not gazing
at the reed wall before me
in the hushed room at dusk.

While I sat straight-backed and still,
one palm gently cupping the other,
following my breaths
in and out as instructed,
my body a small tree
rooted yet open to the world,
to the small breeze
that might rustle my leaves
or rain that might nourish my roots,
before I knew it there he was,
sitting on a branch of that tree,
or rather that idea of tree
I had constructed
instead of observing
those simple breaths.

As many before have discovered,
only in the attempt to still my mind
did I see how busy it was,

thoughts ambling down the sidewalk
chatting among themselves and
making plans for the evening or the next day,
or crossing the street randomly
paying no attention to cross signals
or traffic or the policeman I tried to be,
my white-gloved hand raised futilely in the air.

Often these thoughts are the monkeys
of desire, suggesting we go for a little ride;
others offer a constant critique of the world,
as if I were trying to groom it,
to pick the fleas from its scalp;
while some cackle nastily,
whipping the shit of old traumas
and unresolved conflicts at me
through the bars of their cage.

Whatever its source,
each thought has equal weight
while it squats in my mind:
an idea for a new novel,
a source of fuel that won't pollute,
or that the color of dryer lint
depends on the palette of fabrics.

Let the thoughts pass through you
is the idea, don't buy into them,
even if they hang by their tails
and screech at the top of their lungs,
but as is so often the case,
I find myself offering them
banana after banana.

The story is told
of the monkey stretching
from the branch as far as he can
to grab the reflection
of the moon in water.
So silly, we think, so deluded,
reaching for truth in a handful of light,
as our lives become history
one breath at a time.

But what better than to be that monkey,
so absorbed in his task,
or perhaps the one who sits
by the porous mound of sand,
teasing the ants out onto a stick
and eating them one at a time.

Endangered Species

The Buddhists say that three things
cannot be long hidden:
the sun, the moon, and the truth.

While I long to see the truth
rise in the east and blaze all day,
to be so full and bright in the night sky
that I can almost name the craters on its face,

I fear it is more like the fisher cat,
or the mountain lion, elusive and shadowy,
even like the okapi, limited to one rain forest
in the Republic of the Congo,
its habitat shrinking with each day.

In this age of ignorance and malignant spin,
the truth has a striped rump
to disguise its profile, and
long ears to sense predators.

I approach it patiently, wordlessly,
leaves proffered in my hand,
eager to see its long blue tongue.

How to Survive Right-Wing Extremism

a nearly found poem

When caught in its rip current,
one should not fight it. Rather,
swim parallel to the shoreline
of sanity and coherence
in order to leave it,
as such currents are generally narrow,
only thirty to one hundred feet wide,
so swimming out of one
by swimming parallel
would take only a little energy.

If you see a person caught in one,
yell at them to do likewise.

Floating until the current disperses
into deeper waters
is another method
of surviving such a danger,
but it may leave the swimmer
farther out from shore
and so isn't the recommended solution.

Novena

After seeing all the devotional notices
left on the altar of the classifieds
among the ads for old tools, odd jobs,
and offers for the grinding of stumps,
those candles of thanks for prayers answered
by saints who worked their magic somehow,
even for the thorniest of problems,
I have decided to chant this novena
for the world nine times a day
for the next nine days.

Saint Anthony, I begin with you,
saint of the Lost and Found,
for surely these days we are just so many
old umbrellas, boots, and scarves
gathered down here in the cardboard box
of Earth, having lost our place
or at least our confidence in it:
Please hear our prayer.

Perhaps, Saint Peregrine, our problems
are more like cancers spreading
from city to city, consuming the good
and raising the shortsighted to power,
and so I call upon you too,
your feathers and talons,
for we need all the help we can get:
Please hear our prayer.

Saint Dymphna, I would like to enlist
your aid as well, for as crazy
as things have become in this world,
as anxious and depressed as we are,
it might well take a patron of the insane
to rid us of all our possessions:
Please hear our prayer.

Saint Francis, of course we will need you,
so peaceful, gentle, and wise,
though with all the harm we have
inflicted on your animals and your
Nature, we could hardly be surprised
if you turned your holy back on us
and continued chatting with Saint Clare:
Please hear our prayer.

Because the actions that shape our world
have us all feeling less than we were,
let me add a plea to you, Saint Christopher,
stripped of your title, your very existence
in doubt, reduced now to remnants
of glue on the dashboards of old Chevys,
for I know you can sympathize with our plight:
Please hear our prayer.

As I look around the world,
at its insurmountable hurdles,
its siblings of greed, injustice, and strife,
I see it is the ninth day already
in so many ways, and so it is inevitable
that I turn finally to you, Saint Jude:
We're not all saints down here, of course,
but the good far outnumber the bad,

and though the cause may seem hopeless,
the stumps too hard to remove,
if you could put in a good word for us,
I'm sure we'd all be very grateful:
Please, hear our prayer.

I know that if any of you can come through,
can turn this crazy ship around for us,
I will be the first to add my little haiku
of thanks and devotion to every
newspaper, every bulletin board, and
every highway overpass on the planet—
Lord have mercy on us.

The Flag of Cucumber

May they all be united
under the flag of cucumber.

—COMMENT BY GERALD STERN AT THE
2002 DODGE POETRY FESTIVAL

That is to say, a flag to remind us
of peeling thin scrolls of dark green skin
and releasing the sweet aroma underneath
as we prepare a salad for friends,
not a flag that shows us films
of broken soldiers staring into space,
of peasants running for cover,
of the tightly folded triangle of flag
handed to a widow beneath a veil.

If not cucumber, it could be a flag of garlic,
common to nearly every culture and
celebrating the miracle of a life
reproduced by planting parts of itself.
I can see it, a pale white bulb stitched
on a field of green, flapping in the breeze
above every courthouse and town hall.

You'd think that after all this time
we might have progressed
to at least a flag of salt,
a substance older than any state or tribe,
or perhaps a flag of rain or soil,
causing each year on the vernal equinox
people around the world to parade as one

behind marching bands and twirled batons
or a procession of wooden flutes and guitars
ending in fields at the edge of town
for the ritual planting of seeds.

Instead we have flags of blind obedience,
flags of lies as shiny as lapel pins,
flags wielded like clubs to hammer the weak,
flags of countries, of regions, of states,
of towns, of teams, even flags of houses,
as if separating ourselves from others
were somehow a source of strength.

So far in our history the flags of loss,
the flags of mourning, the flags of regret
and even of shame have not been enough
to bring us to our senses, and
we have forgotten every pledge we've made.
I fear it may come down to the flag of disease
or the flag of drought, or the flag
of poisoned water that finally unites us.

I would like it to be different, is all.
I won't pretend it could be the flag of love,
so volatile it snaps in the slightest breeze,
or the flag of any god, when dogmas
don't seem to deliver us from evil.
But surely there is something to salute
that contains liberty and justice for all.

Whatever symbol future humans choose
for their flag, after the nonsense is over,
let the fabric come from some fiber of corn, or rice,
and let the flag be burned without complaint,
for heat, or just for the pretty flame.

2

Memoir

1

With each hat that Bartholomew Cubbins removed,
I trembled under the bedclothes, identifying more deeply
with his predicament. If he could not remove his hat
for the king, his head would be chopped off
by a masked executioner with an ax as broad as his chest,
or be pushed off the castle tower to his death, or who knows
what worse torture lurked on the next page,
all of it certified by my mother or father
spooning it to my ears.

Yet with each hat he took off, or was knocked off
by wind, or was shot off by the Yeoman of the Bowmen,
whose "bow was as big as the branch of a tree,"
another hat appeared, as it can in books and the mind,
and even so young I knew at least in my bones
that the hat was more than a hat, that one day,
for no apparent reason, fears and worries
just wouldn't come off so easily
at the end of a day, even a simple day
of selling cranberries at the market.

Later I could say that Dr. Seuss was Kafka for kids,
with its pages without page numbers, its protagonist
accused of an obscure and meaningless crime,
but I learned right then that although the king
might eventually give you gold for an absurd reason,

the answers to your real questions could not be pulled
from any hat, and the events of your life
were arbitrary arrows shot by God, and no one
"in the Kingdom of Didd could ever explain
how a strange thing had happened. They only
could say it just 'happened to happen'
and was not very likely to happen again."

2

At ten or so, the Hardy Boys rescued me
in their yellow convertible. Mysteries were nothing
but sport to them, and they solved about one a week,
or as fast as I could devour the numbered titles
in order: *The Tower Treasure, The House on the Cliff,
The Secret of the Old Mill, The Missing Chums.*

In the fifty-eight I read, they never aged;
apparently one could float on the inner tube
of adolescence out on Barmet Bay as long as one liked.
They lived in Bayport, in a two-story Victorian
on the corner of Elm Street with their father, Fenton,
mother, Laura, Aunt Gertrude, and
the Dutch philosopher Spinoza.

Like Spinoza, they spent their day "sleuthing,"
teaching me with each book that any mystery
could be solved if the mind were large enough.
A novel confirms there is no free will, especially
upon rereading. Our lives are driven by plots
that must happen the way they do. The truth
may use a red wig to disguise itself, or
wear someone else's shoes to cover its tracks,
but as their father the famous detective said,
"One bit of success makes up for a hundred false trails."

As for the past, which at age ten I was beginning
to realize existed, according to Frank and Joe,
you could "press your ear to the ground
and listen for receding footsteps."

3

The summer after high school,
after my father's near-fatal heart attack
had knocked out one of my pillars of certainty,
when my draft number was forty
and crazy Richard Nixon sat in an oval office
deciding whether or not to send me to Da Nang,
Catch-22 made perfect sense.

"Each day you faced was another dangerous mission
against mortality," as Yossarian said,
with the flak of disasters and diseases
bursting all around you, and faith
was a parachute that might not open.
Good and evil were two whores
who stripped on a whim to reveal the other;
sanity was a mask that most people
didn't know they were wearing.
"There was no way of really knowing anything,"
the novel suggested, "not even that
there was no way of really knowing anything."

You might stanch the wounds of these discoveries
with sulfanilamide, or dull the pain with morphine,
but in the end, courage still existed, and
if you had to ditch your plane in such uncharted waters,
you could try rowing to freedom
with the tiny blue oars of irony and humor.

Three semesters in, I dropped out of college,
unsure of my place or path, like a drifter
standing on a corner in an old Western
who takes odd jobs while he plans his next move.
First I made cardboard slabs for the world
all through the night, then guarded
barrels of powdered onion and garlic
that went into A1 sauce, then shivered
through a pointless strike in the middle of winter
because it was my union's turn.
After four years in the wilderness, after
I had washed my old school clothes,
I returned, and stumbled into a class
where in my hands lay panned gold:
Walker Percy's *The Moviegoer.*

Yes, we live "on an insignificant cinder
spinning away in a dark corner of the universe,"
surrounded by a strip-mall world
where people are "locked in a death grip
with everydayness," everyone at risk
of becoming an Anyone living Anywhere,
and yes, malaise can chase you like the posse
in a movie stirring up dust across the valley,
"a little tongue of hellfire licking at your heels."

But reading about a man in despair
was not the same as being a man in despair.
It was possible to find yourself on a Search,
to remember from the movies that the drifter
was usually on to something, and to the seeker
things could "look both unfamiliar
and at the same time full of clues."

Not only did Percy certify my search,
he said my life depended on it,
to avoid becoming an automaton or a ghost.
No matter what stagecoach I found myself on,
if I were always on the alert
for "the singularities of time and place,"
I could be "out in the world, out
in the thick summer air between sky and earth,"
where there was never a moment without wonder.

More

I am two years old
in the black-and-white snapshot,
out in the backyard
at the end of a length of clothesline
my mother used as a leash
when she was busy inside.
The whole radius of yard,
with its cluster of daylilies,
its sandbox, its lawn of fascinating beetles,
is evidently not enough, as in the picture
I lean out beyond the limit of the rope
trying to smell a rose.

My first sentence, they told me,
was "Outdoors more," followed by
"Go car more." (Once, at four,
in my first good advice to my type A
father, I told him, "Sit down more.")

As a teenager not old enough to work,
I stayed up a little later each summer night
wringing more out of the day
until the week before school started again
I was up till nearly dawn,
when I knew the previous day officially ends,
and I often had two or three fires going at once
as if by watching a Jimmy Cagney movie
while computing baseball stats while
eating pizza I could somehow scoop
extra time from a finite pool.

Now as an adult, I feel that spice amounts
in recipes are like placebos,
that seedlings don't really need to be thinned,
that encores and extra innings
quicken the pulse of life.

Of course I've seen the dangers of more:
twisted heaps of metal between
flashing lights on the highway;
my father trying at age seventy
to drink only on Mondays and Thursdays;
my friend years ago who wound a shoelace
around his arm to raise a better vein.
These are full-length mirrors to me.

I know too that this is the kind of living
that leads one away from enlightenment,
that the idea is to empty, not fill,
to release and not grasp,
that the rose will still be there
when I am finally untied.

But when death comes,
I will probably want more of that too,
more speed rushing down the tunnel
and a brighter, whiter light at the end,
the place where will is ground to sawdust,
where desire becomes vapor,
all yearning sloughs away.

Or will I resist that
Church of Sufficient Grace,
its humble white clapboards, shingled roof,
and two wooden steps up to the front door,
will I still beg for dessert,
a nightcap, another helping of life?

Plasticville

I zip home from work in my dark green,
open cockpit Lotus, squealing around
the lichen trees at Forest and Main,
turn left at Racetrack Lane
and cross over the tracks,
then pull into the vast parking area
next to my tiny ranch house
with pastel-blue roof
and matching garage door,
parking the Lotus in its slot
next to the green Aston Martin,
the red E-Type Jaguar,
the Triumph motorcycle with sidecar,
the Volkswagen Caravette van
with green-tinted windows,
and the Aveling-Barford tractor shovel.
The house's front door is stuck, as if glued shut,
and so I just peer inside the windows
at the darkened, empty rooms.

It was a tough day at work,
at whatever it is I do,
and it makes me want to take the Maserati,
glinting in what passes for sun
in its special spot by the side of the house,
out for a spin around town, past the Church,
the Bank, the School, the Five-and-Ten, the Gas Station,
then out into the giant ball field where in the outfield
I turn wicked donuts that leave no mark.

From above, the world looks flat
and uniformly green
as if paint on a sheet of plywood,
the edges of town menacing
in their precipitous drop off all four sides.
This is Plasticville
says the name on the Railroad Station
I snapped together long ago,
and also on the Bank, the School,
and everything else in the rectangular town
on the netless Ping-Pong table
in the cellar of my childhood,
the temperature here a steady sixty-five,
with no chance of rain or even a breeze.

We never called it that, though, Plasticville,
we neighborhood boys who built these worlds
in our cellars, always just the City,
a refuge from the summer heat
and for me, I guess, a respite from the tug-of-war
silences my parents called a marriage.

It is hard to believe the hundreds of hours
I spent in that world come back so vaguely,
even after I spot the Matchbox Lotus for sale on eBay,
mint with original box for nine dollars plus shipping,
the decal number 3s still intact on each side.

I know we invented our lives as best we could,
trying to extract experiences from material things,
discussing our cars, shuffling houses and stores,
even repainting our cars with shiny Testors paint,
then adding a slot-car track for more to do,
yet how many times around that slot-car figure eight
that wound through town before it was just a finger
tracing infinity again and again.

We pretended to be adults, of course,
as if grown-up responsibilities consisted of
speeding around town in expensive sports cars
all day long, even as we saw our own fathers
trudge up the walk after work, then
slump in a chair with a scotch.

In another year or two we'd learn
that some people did drop off the edge
when they left town, for Khe Sanh or Dien Bien Phu,
or they found the other dark and empty rooms
of divorce, or addiction, or despair.

But for a time in our lives, in the City
at least, anyone involved in a crash
made an instant, cartoon recovery,
and order in the world was achieved easily
by lining up your vehicles in a row
or polishing the contacts on your slot cars
with emery cloth until they shone.

When the Lotus comes in the mail,
I race it around my desk,
making engine sounds in my throat
and tire squeals on the impossible turn
around my coffee mug, then back it in
between my watch and a stack of bills.

Honorary Junior Black Panther

Summer, 1970

1

"The Revolution starts tonight," he growled
into the back of my head, having jumped and pinned me
to the ground just before midnight, rubbing my face
in the dirt. I responded as anyone in my situation might:

"Victor, get off me."

"Who's this Victor?" he grunted, and I realized then
he was trying to disguise his voice.

It might seem surprising that the Revolution,
with capital *R,* would begin just outside the latrine
at a summer camp in the Maine woods,
but to Victor and his friends, refugees from the City,
with capital *C,* by day just other junior counselors
to poor kids bussed in from Gardiner and Hallowell,
by night junior Black Panthers with power salutes
and ongoing rhetoric jousts about Bobby and Huey
and overthrowing the state we heard as we passed
their cabin, it made perfect sense. Victor saw through
my long-haired, protest-the-war facade,
his trained eyes revealing what I was,
a privileged white suburban Connecticut rat.

It was practice, of course, guerrilla war games,
with slim pickings for potential victims

out in the middle of nowhere, and after a while
of trading the same lines of dialogue back and forth,
he let me up. It might seem that at age fifteen
I played a small role in the dominant oppressive
power structure of the United States,
but I guess you have to start somewhere.

2

At Camp Ridgeway we boarded an old school bus
each week for our only excursion into civilization:
laundry, at a little strip mall in Augusta.
While it agitated, in twos and fours we roamed
the aisles of the Zayre department store next door,
our mixed races, long hair, and hippy clothes a magnet
for the plain-clothed but obvious security guards
in their nearly matching green plaid shirts
who followed us up and down the aisles,
tossing one odd item from each department
into their carriages: a toaster, argyle socks, a lawn chair.

One week waiting for a friend at the checkout
I witnessed the assembled clerks, mostly bored
high school girls, snickering and pointing
at an odd-looking couple who left the store
embarrassed and obviously hurt. Righteousness
possessed me, and I stepped up to the ringleader:
"That was a bastard thing to do," I said,
then harangued her as I clicked staples from her stapler
as if emptying bullets from a chamber.

Apparently the men in plaid saw this,
and after we all got back to the Laundromat,
within minutes the real police arrived, aiming

to stamp out this insurrection before it spread,
the gung-ho sergeant drawling with a jarring
southern accent, "You know ah ought
to arrest you, young mayan."

After twenty minutes of circular, fruitless interrogation
as the last of our tie-dyed shirts and frayed jeans
finished their spin cycle behind me,
they banned me from Zayre,
one of the great disappointments of my life.

Back on the bus for the ride back to camp,
my fellow counselors reveling in my brush with the Man,
who should come striding down the aisle
but Victor, his wild ringlets dancing on his shoulders.
He stopped in front of me, slapped me
a soul handshake, and said, "Way to go, bro',"
as if pinning on me a merit badge for Valor.

Panning

June 1, 1980

Happy to get any ride across the Mojave Desert,
my friend and I tossed our packs into the back
of the pickup truck and rode the waves of highway
from Flagstaff to Vegas fried by the wind and sun
in the high thin air. The truck bed was filled
with the couple's meager belongings collected
in garbage bags we used for pillows,
and a carton of old milk rotting in the sun.
On stops for gas and once for a flat tire
we learned their story: Gerald, with bad teeth
and bare feet and long, dirty fingernails, wearing
a silver bull pendant, had lost his job in Texas
but was full of his plan to move to Oregon,
to pan for gold and shoot porcupines for money—
"a dollar a head, and you can kill two hundred in a night."
They had already hocked their TV and chairs for gas money
and now were down to a laundry sack of coins
they'd saved to play the penny and nickel slots in Nevada.

He said all of it brightly, but with a twist in his eye
that made us wonder once when they stopped at a gas station
but didn't get out, just stopped, if the plan included
my friend and me jumping out together to use the bathroom
and never seeing our packs again, or if the knife
in the sheath strapped to his thigh
was more than a cowboy prop.

Late in the ride, late in the story, as we passed by towns
named Chloride and Grasshopper Junction, mostly scrub
as far as the eye could see, as our transient family
chugged toward the sights of the Hoover Dam,
the woman rapped on the thin window separating us
and pointed down, into the trash below us, smiling.
We rooted around for anything of value or meaning
until my friend held up a box of Pampers. She smiled
and nodded, and as he passed one around to her window
at sixty miles an hour it dawned on us that all along
on the front seat had been a tiny baby
gurgling its trust in their great adventure.

General Lee

for Jim LaPenta

We buried General Lee in a shallow grave
at the edge of a cornfield on a commanding hill,
wrapped in a Confederate flag once stolen
from a store in Pennsylvania.
We covered the grave with a flagstone slab
the shape of Virginia.

We drank a beer, talked about
Little Tennessee, Shiloh, Purple Haze,
and other cats we've known.
A breeze changed the shadows around us.

I couldn't help recalling the night
I buried Rough Edges, an old stray
who'd taken to lounging atop my woodpile
under the slanted roof out back,
who died in his sleep one day
on a scrap of yellow carpet
I'd put there to cushion his hard life.

I couldn't find a shovel, and it took
two hours in a steady drizzle
to dig a good grave with my garden trowel
in the rocky soil down by the Mount Hope River.
A cat deserves a good grave.

I told my friend not to blame himself
for General Lee's demise, that he'd had
to move somewhere, and cats get hit.

He thanked me for the stone and my time,
and I went home to nuzzle the fur
of the best cat I ever had,
who absorbed my affections
without another thought.

Grief

Having known grief before, I expected
the heaviness in the chest,
the low, slow, shallow breaths you notice
before the long inhalation and the sigh,
so needed. I expected the ghosts,
her curled in a ball against
the arm of the love seat for a second,
the flash of her striped rump and tail
disappearing through a doorway.

And in the mathematics of the house
with an indoor cat, the absence of her
in the rooms downstairs *meant*
the presence of her elsewhere,
so as I climb the stairs and realize she is not
stretched out on the northwest corner
of the bed to catch the afternoon sun,
or on my soft desk chair, expecting me,
it jars. There is a dizziness.

But after eighteen years of this
deepening consonance, the surprise
I feel most is in the texture of her spotted belly fur,
the chin slowly rotating against my scratching fingers,
the simple heft of her as the vacant claws
knead my shoulder through a flannel shirt—
all so present in my aching cells.

Birthday

"I'm in labor with you!" my wife shouts at her daughter,
stopped cold in the upstairs hall at 7 P.M. December 2nd,
three hours before she arrives thirteen years ago.

She can't help it. She knows that soon Giulia will come out
blue, four pounds and change, not even breathing right away,
that she won't be allowed to hold her, and her first touch
will be through plastic mitts that snake into a chamber
puffing the first air of a new planet into her bean-sized lungs.
"I didn't know what else to do," she tells me,
"so I petted her like a little cat."

Even taking the tiny ski cap topped with holly from the box
in the attic, still bloodstained, holding it in her hand,
imagining the creature whose bottom fit in one palm,
won't relax her contractions of fear.

Staring at the blooming youngster now before her in the hall,
wide-eyed and beautiful, as tall as she is, hardly convinces her
of the miracle until Giulia, as if slapped, cries, "Mom,
don't yell at me. I'm not born yet!"

The Country of Bed

While I work at my desk, shuffling bills
and rummaging through stacks of papers
and books, my wife slips into the room.

It is July, yet chilly this cloudy afternoon.
She presses the swollen door into the frame,
far enough to discourage any cat or child

from breaking its seal. She lies down on the bed,
her "country of bed," and sighs as she pulls a quilt
over her body to her chin. Within a minute or two,

she softly snores, the way a cat snores,
a little engine in the room you weren't aware of
till now. A gentle rain burbles down the gutters,

and soon I am a captive: to open the door
to bring my work downstairs would wake her;
to rise from my chair, with its two sharp metal

creaks, impossible. Even sorting papers seems noisy
inside this place. I feel my fingers tensed
on the desk, sense the urgency in my elbows' angles,

and then take a deep breath. I exhale thoughts of
task task task being crossed off the master list
and find myself breathing inside a small moment,

a balloon of time lifting from the linear world.
A book of essays by Charles Simic is within reach,
and I open to a description of eating ripe tomatoes.

His prose transports me, quiet as a spy. Soon,
without my bidding, these words seep out of my hand,
a purple finger with a ballpoint spreading them

across this yellow page, the only sound the scuff
of my hand as it lifts every two or three words,
like surf on some distant shore.

The Paddle

for Marian

To the music
of gulls and terns
we set out
in our kayak for two

to cross the bay
shimmering
like a newly waxed floor.

This is our dance, dear,
the one I promised you.

Here there is no confusion
of steps
or stepping on feet
and we lead by turns.

And if once in a while
our paddles clash
like cymbals
in the wrong measure

we apologize
and regain our rhythm
in a few strokes.

Let no one else
tap the shoulder
of your affection,
my love.

Let us continue this
dip and turn, dip
and turn.

The News

I step out of the grocery store
with my milk and juice, some ripe bananas,
a home magazine for my wife,
and walk back to my car
as others pass me with their lists,
their intentions and duties,
and the thought comes from nowhere,
again, that the news could be waiting for me,
like a coiled snake,
that my wife has suddenly died.

I am the last person on Earth
without a cell phone
so it may be a while before I find out.
I may fill the car with gas,
not knowing, may wait at a red light,
not knowing, buy strawberries at the stand,
still asleep in life's quotidian trance,
traveling without irony
as I plan our dinner together,
pouring the wine in my mind,
nestling with her on our red couch,
settling in for a movie or the game.

It won't take as long as it did
for the sailor stepping off the ship
in a distant port after a thousand miles at sea,
or the settler building a house
at the edge of the wilderness,

the news arriving weeks or even months
after the awful event, in a crumpled envelope
lifted from a black leather sack,
but it will come soon enough,
as I turn onto our street and see way down
the flashing lights in front of what I pray
is not our house, or perhaps not until
I reach the house, and see the blinking
phone machine for the last time without dread.

I have tried changing the subject, or
pretending the thought isn't there,
but we exist at the mercy of our imaginations,
which know not what they do, and so it is no use.
The thought knocks, and I must answer,
allow the thing in, its reality assuming form
and dimension as my heartbeat quickens,
purpose and meaning sucked with me
into the whirlpool of grief
from which I know there will be no return.

The news is so huge
I can only take in a tiny part of it,
thank god,
and now, stopped in traffic,
I turn my face to the sun,
imagine that it has gone out,
and that in eight minutes that news
will reach the Earth, enough time
for me to bask in the sun's wisdom,
contained in these strawberries,
this cloth seat, these fingers
gripping the wheel, even that truck
moving out of my path
as I rush home.

Development

Across the lake from this cottage
on a morning perfectly still
except for tiny ripples sent to shore
by diving loons, an occasional clown-step
by a great blue heron fishing in the shallows,
the light magnified by thousands of mirrors
that compose the surface of the water,
a morning so perfect you could not ask for it,
someone is clearing trees with a chainsaw,
revving its engine like a motorcycle,
so that someone else, most likely,
can sit on the porch of their new house
on a morning perfectly still except for
tiny ripples sent to the shore by loons.

Good Days

"Most of the days were good,"
wrote the stranger who rented this cottage
the week before us, meaning it didn't rain,
even though the whole area is suffering from drought
and all the wells are beginning to run dry.

The day in 1980 when Mount Saint Helens erupted,
sending fifty-seven people to their deaths
and wiping out forty-seven bridges
and miles and miles of highway, was bad,

though the sunset I saw three days later
in Colorado carried, as a result,
the most beautiful streaks of purple
I have seen, and the ash that dusted
the backs of cows in Washington
and Oregon, though it ruined carburetors
for miles, turned out to enrich the soil
for years to come.

Surely someone cursed himself
for sleeping through his alarm
or got into an extended fight with his wife
or even rear-ended a Jaguar
trying to get to work in the towers
on September 11th.

Even Hitler's order in August of 1939
for his armies to invade Poland
might have caused two refugees

from different cities to meet
in an abandoned barn and fall in love.

And I don't have to tell you the days
when the combustion engine and plastic
were invented didn't turn out to be
as great as they seemed at the time.

Moments ride the seesaw of history
with its fulcrum of fate so often
that I'm not sure I even know
what a good day is anymore,

but I think I'll take my chances
with the two of us staring out
across this lake at dusk, clinking
our glasses of zinfandel together
as the lights on the opposite shore blink on.

The Art of Memory

I didn't miss cappuccino at all.
It was the idea I missed . . .
the idea of cappuccino.

—MARTHA STEWART, ON HER RELEASE FROM JAIL

Not the sweet-bitter liquid
going down my throat,
not the hint of cinnamon froth
on my top lip, not the exchange of bill
for coins with another human being

but all of that experience
somehow contained now
in a cell of my brain,
its luster diminished a bit
each time in the visiting room
there, where we may
stare at each other through
wire-meshed glass but not touch.

And it is like so many ideas
that were once things, or people,
living now in the giant cave of memory,
at the end of one long chamber the lobster bake
in the beach on Vinalhaven Island,
lobsters, corn, and mussels filling a sandwich
of seaweed and hot stones,
when Joey Plisga and I
went from table to table
cracking lobsters with knowing twists
for kids from New York

who gave us a claw apiece,
at least the way I've been telling it
the last thirty-eight years.

Or the very short tunnel
I started digging just last night
at the restaurant in Rockland
after visiting the museum:
the olive boat, the marinated lamb,
the chocolate fondue with its grapes,
apple wedges, strawberries,
and cubes of bread.
This morning I find the experience
is already sorting itself.

The myths of photography
and the vivid charades of film
can be convincing, but I admire instead
the chemical bath of the mind
and how it develops events and scenes
over time like the artist it is,
arranging all neatly into narrative
and lyric, so confident of its own truths,

as now I fix the gaze
of my spelunker's lamp
on the tiny dot of an orange spider
zooming across this blank white page
and smear its neon life
into something like history.

The Next-to-Last Poem

One more minute in this scented garden
surrounded by curious, intelligent people
listening to a fellow soul navigate the chaos
of existence with only the kayak of language
is suddenly more than they can bear.

They rise at the announcement of penultimeity
as if hearing the starter's pistol, or the Wall Street bell,
begin compressing the chair, or snapping the blanket
free of its grass confetti, forcing those behind them
to bob and weave for peeks at the podium.

Their lives are so important, their activities
jigged together inside such a grid,
the fact that all the last poems they've missed
would fill a great anthology means nothing to them,
the insult to the poets just so much dirt
kicked off their shoes as they climb into their cars,
nothing in life so gratifying as beating the traffic.

Like those who sneak out of Mass right after
Communion, the host not yet dissolved on their tongues,
they have no shame. But as the priest would say,
their Communion is incomplete, and they'll have
to get by somehow without the benediction.

The Almanac

I take it down from the shelf and sit in my favorite chair,
admire the grain of the imitation black leather, run my finger
over the bumps of the gold letters that spell my name.
I open to the chapter on Marian, my wife:
>   first sighting, it says,
>   Pero's Fruit Stand, September 9, 1961, 9:14 A.M.
Both seven years old and out with our fathers, I guess,
on a Saturday morning.
I can imagine it but not remember it.
>   number of times our paths crossed
>   before we knew each other: eleven,
>   including Woodland Gardens, four times,
>   each with year, month, and day;
>   the old State Theatre on Main Street, twice
>   (*The Time Machine, Mary Poppins*);
>   Reed's bookstore in the Parkade, once
>   (for me, *The Shore Road Mystery*, it notes;
>   for her, *The Whispering Statue*).
A footnote says I received one of her nickels in change.

I thumb through the book, pause at the chapter on "The Body."
The print is small, like a Bible's, the pages very thin.
I glance through the statistics,
updated since I last closed the book:
>   number of hairs lost, number remaining,
>   number of moles and freckles in the constellation,
>   length of toe- and fingernails grown, total, in feet.
I skim through the history section, scan my diseases:
>   polio,
>   mumps,

measles,
>tonsillitis (and the date tonsils removed),
>colds and flus,
>the occasional food poisoning,
>cancer.

Many of these I do remember. It reads like a living obituary,
a genre to which I am always drawn. I read the chronicles
of strangers every day, piecing their lives together
from the scarce detail the newspaper supplies.
Here is the foot-deep accumulation of facts I desire,
enough to slow me down just wading through them.
At the end of the chapter, a favorite:

>current global distribution of air molecules
>my lungs have filtered since birth.

By list, graph, and map, most impressive.
Three have been to the moon.

Under "Lineage," a chapter I can't stay away from
even though it never changes, I read once more
page after page of my ancestors. Only the first page,
with the book turned sideways, is able to hold a chart,
the names a binomial explosion. This is a chapter
both clear and dizzying. At a mere fifteen generations back,
each of my forebears is named and placed,
yet 32,768 of them live in tiny letters I can barely make out
with the magnifying glass I keep on my side table for that purpose.
They come from eleven countries, clusters of names from the same towns,
many names the same, as I am related and re-related
to people I can never know beyond

>"John Porter, Essex, England, 1594–1648,"
>an antecedent by four different paths.

I picture him hunched over his hoe,
turning over another lump of sandstone,
now straightening to wipe the sweat from his eyes.
It is well past noon, and he is very thirsty.
He can little imagine the genes of thousands conspiring even then

to produce my genetic code, and neither can I.
I am glad the genealogical trail stops abruptly for lack of space,
not sure I could handle the 1,048,576 names the book tells me
would be listed for the twentieth generation back.

Quickly immersing myself in chapter 9, "Food,"
I am once again humbled, grateful, and guilty
at the number of
> chickens,
>
> cows,
>
> pigs,
>
> salmon,
>
> cod,
>
> mussels,
>
> and lobsters

I have evidently gorged myself on.
Shamed by the thousands of miles
all the out-of-season strawberries have traveled,
the barrels of oil and gas consumed to ferry them,
I am reminded of the section I studied last week,
the number of workers by country who have stitched my shirts,
laced my shoes, turned the legs of my chair.
I reflect soberly on the wine and spirits, listed in gallons,
pat myself on the back for the bushels of
> broccoli,
>
> chard,
>
> kale,
>
> and other greens consumed.

Once again I realize just what a factory I am,
what a sieve, what a universe, and what a cog,
as all the cross-references collect in a heap at the end of the chapter:
> sources of water for all this raising and growing,
>
> repositories of waste,
>
> poisons distributed,
>
> and money, always money, changing hands.

It is nearly time for bed, time to add to the number of dreams
and dream characters (see chapter 18), the breaths both in and out,
the heartbeats climbing toward their final tally.
I look in the index under "Lodging, places slept."
On page 512 I find the exhaustive list of
> apartments,
> houses,
> hotels,
> motels,
> cabins,
> campgrounds (58),
> dorm rooms (7),
> hospitals (2),
> parking lots (1, Gary, Indiana),
> and ditches (also 1, Julesburg, Colorado).

I close the book and return it to its slot on the shelf.
When I shut off the light, I can still see the silhouette
of my third cat, curled in a ball against the bump of my wife's leg
under the covers of my fourth bed. I pause
to survey this landscape by the light of my only moon.